IMAGES
of America

CRATER LAKE
NATIONAL PARK

IMAGES
of America

CRATER LAKE
NATIONAL PARK

Margaret LaPlante

ARCADIA
PUBLISHING

Published by Arcadia Publishing
Charleston, South Carolina

Printed in the United States of America

Library of Congress Control Number: 2013941008

For all general information, please contact Arcadia Publishing:
Telephone 843-853-2070
Fax 843-853-0044
E-mail sales@arcadiapublishing.com
For customer service and orders:
Toll-Free 1-888-313-2665

Visit us on the Internet at www.arcadiapublishing.com

*This book is dedicated to everyone who has
worked at Crater Lake over the years.*

CONTENTS

ACKNOWLEDGMENTS

The historical images in this book are courtesy of the Crater Lake National Park Museum and Archives collections.

INTRODUCTION

The Cascade Range of volcanoes runs from Mount Garibaldi in Canada all the way down to Mount Lassen in California. The plateau base of this range came into being when the earth's crust folded and lifted upwards. Soon after, molten rock pushed toward the surface, which caused eruptions, and lava welled up through the cracks in the surface.

One of the volcanoes along the Cascade Range, Mount Mazama, was located in southern Oregon. For more than half a million years, Mount Mazama produced eruptions that put forth pumice, ash, and cinders into the air. Over time, magma vents and cones developed on the mass of the volcano, which weakened its structure. About 7,700 years ago, the volcano had such a massive eruption that it could no longer support itself and collapsed, leaving a huge caldera. Over time, there were additional rumblings, which is how Wizard Island and the Merriam cones came into existence. They are considered volcanoes within a volcano. It has been more than 5,000 years since the last rumblings of this great volcano.

At first, the surface of the caldera was too hot to hold water, but eventually the volcanic action subsided. Over the past centuries, the caldera filled with rain and melted snow. Today, that caldera is known as Crater Lake. It is the deepest lake in the United States, with a maximum depth of 1,943 feet. The depth of the lake remains fairly stable between evaporation and new precipitation. In an average year, the depth does not change more than three feet.

The caldera is nearly circular in shape and stretches roughly six miles across at its widest point. The area of the lake covers approximately 20 square miles. The lake is surrounded by almost 26 miles of lava cliffs, which are the remains of Mount Mazama. The cliffs range in height from 500 feet to 2,000 feet above the surface of the water. The elevation at the lake level is 6,173 feet.

The deep-blue water changes as light is absorbed, color by color, as it passes through the water. The color red passes through the water first, followed by orange, yellow, and green. The color blue is the last color to be absorbed by the water. This creates the deep-blue water that Crater Lake is known for. There is no inlet or outlet, so the water in Crater Lake remains pure.

Those who call Crater Lake home include black bears, black-tailed deer, elk, red foxes, coyotes, cougars, pine martens, bobcats, pronghorns, porcupines, ground squirrels, and yellow-bellied marmots. There are more than 120 species of birds in the park, including American bald eagles. More than 570 species of flowering plants and ferns bring beauty to the area.

It is believed that humans have lived in this area for more than 10,000 years. Therefore, it is likely humans witnessed the eruption of Mount Mazama. Some of the first white men to explore the area were fur traders. But things began to change in the 1840s. A few parties set out to explore the land that Lewis and Clark had seen for the first time decades prior. Soon, others followed and eventually the Gold Rush and the Donation Land Claim brought hundreds of thousands westward.

The first authenticated white man to see the caldera was John W. Hillman in 1853. Hillman was 17 years old when he left his home in Albany, New York, and made his way out west with his father, hoping to strike it rich in the 1849 California Gold Rush. His quest led him, along with 11 other men, including, in part, Isaac G. Skeeters, a Mr. Dodd, James L. Loudon, Patrick McManus, George Ross, and Henry Klippel, to the Cascade Mountains. They were searching for the "Lost Cabin Mine." Realizing they had lost their way, they decided to climb the nearest peak so they could establish their whereabouts. It was there on June 12, 1853, that they gazed down on what would later be known as Crater Lake.

Years later, Hillman described the amazement he felt in seeing such a magnificent sight: "On the evening of the first day, while riding up a long, sloping mountain, we suddenly came in sight of water, and were very much surprised, as we did not expect to see any lakes, and did not know but what we had come in sight of, and close to Klamath Lake, and not until my mule stopped within a few feet of the rim of Crater Lake did I look down, and if I had been riding a blind mule I firmly believe I would have ridden over the edge to death and destruction. We came to the lake a very little to the right of a small sloping butte or mountain, situated in the lake, with a top somewhat flattened. Every man of the party gazed with wonder at the sight before him, and each in his own peculiar way gave expression to the thoughts within him, but we had no time to lose, and after rolling some boulders down the side of the lake, we rode to the left, as near the rim as possible, past the butte, looking to see an outlet for the lake, but we could find none. I was very anxious to find a way to the water, which was immediately vetoed by the whole party, and as the leader of the Californians had become discouraged, we decided to return to camp; but not before we discussed what name we should give the lake. There were many names suggested, but Mysterious Lake and Deep Blue Lake were most favorably received, and on a vote, Deep Blue Lake was chosen for a name."

William Gladstone Steel first laid eyes on Crater Lake on August 15, 1885. Originally from Ohio, he was living in Portland when he made his first trip to the lake. He was accompanied by friends J.M. Breck, Capt. Clarence E. Dutton from Fort Klamath, and Joseph LeConte, a geologist from the University of California, Berkeley. Years later, he recalled that first trip: "Not a foot of the land about the lake had been touched or claimed. An overmastering conviction came to me that this wonderful spot must be saved, wild and beautiful, just as it was, for all future generations, and that it was up to me to do something. I then and there had the impression that in some way, I didn't know how, the lake ought to become a National Park. I was so burdened with the idea that I was distressed. Many hours in Captain Dutton's tent, we talked of plans to save the lake from private exploitation. We discussed its wonders, mystery and inspiring beauty, its forests and strange lava structure. The captain agreed with the idea that something ought to be done, and done at once if the lake was to be saved, and that it should be made a National Park." What Steel could not have imagined that night was it would take 17 years for that dream to become a reality.

At Steel's urging, Pres. Grover Cleveland signed an executive order on February 1, 1886, which temporarily withdrew 10 townships of public land around Crater Lake from settlement or sale. The townships were to be "dedicated and set apart forever as a public park or pleasure ground and forest reserve for the benefit of the people of the United States." This was done in anticipation of formally creating a national park. However, there was much opposition from those who feared the loss of timber and mining rights. Ranchers complained of the loss of land to graze their cattle. To make their point, a group of ranchers placed 2,000 sheep in the vicinity and allowed them to graze. Their protests were short-lived when a United States marshal arrested the ranchers.

In an effort to learn more about the lake and the surrounding area, Steel returned to the lake in July 1886, this time with boats so he could explore the body of water. He traveled by train to Ashland, where he met up with Captains Dutton and Davis and a number of soldiers. Together, they set off for Crater Lake with three double teams, horsemen, and a pack team carrying a 26-foot-long boat Steel named *Cleetwood*. They also had a lapstrake boat that was carried by a four-mule team. Steel remembered that as they passed through the town of Phoenix, a young lad stood by the road and predicted that the boat would never hold up because "it had been made by someone who had never seen a boat before."

The men reached the lake and began preparations for getting the boat down to the water. They made a sled from timbers, then lashed the *Cleetwood* to the sled. They placed ropes on the corners of the sled to control the speed of the descent. Steel recalled the excitement of the launching: "On Saturday morning I stood on a snow bank with a watch in my hand and every man in his place. At exactly 8 o'clock I gave the word and all jumped to their positions and the serious launching was underway. For eight hours without stopping to eat or otherwise, 16 men labored with every nerve strained in an earnest desire to do his best. Then we found ourselves at the foot of the canyon, with *Cleetwood*'s nose projecting over an embankment 10 feet high, directly over the water, and not a foot of cable to be had. The oars were secured in the boat, a man sat in the stern bracing himself as best he could. With a single stroke the cable was cut, the boat shot forward and down and the man gathered himself up in the bow with blood upon his face and bruised all over, but the happiest man in Oregon, for, had he not driven the mules that drew the *Cleetwood* 100 miles into the mountains and finished the trip on the water?"

They enjoyed a short tour of the water that day and then spent the next several days exploring the entire lake. Using piano wire, they sounded the lake 168 times and concluded that the deepest point was 1,996 feet.

Upon being on the water for the first time, Steel reported "the scenery was grand to a degree far beyond our most sanguine expectations. Four strong oarsmen soon brought us to Llao Rock and as we gazed in silent wonder at its rugged sides, reaching nearly half a mile above us, for the first time did we realize the immensity of such a spectacle." During their time on the water, Steel named several of the lake's prominent features, including Wizard Island, "because of its weird appearance" and its resemblance to a wizard's hat. The crater at the top was named the Witch's Cauldron.

On his way home to Portland, Steel stopped by the Honorable Binger Hermann's house in Roseburg; Hermann was an Oregon congressman. They spoke at length about the possibility of creating a national park. Hermann agreed to assist Steel in his quest for to make Crater Lake a national park.

Every time things looked promising, one group or another would vehemently oppose the idea of a national park and Steel would be defeated. There were years when the House of Representatives would approve the bill to create a national park, only to have the bill defeated in the Senate.

The years went by and Steel continued to fight for Crater Lake to become a national park, but the opposition stood firm. Those opposed feared the loss of logging, mining rights, and sheep grazing and could not understand the benefit of tourism is such a remote spot.

In 1901, Oregon congressman Thomas Tongue introduced a bill to make Crater Lake a national park. There was still plenty of opposition, but this time there was a glimmer of hope. This encouraged Steel, who immediately began a media campaign. He circulated a statewide petition. He campaigned that "adjoining the lake and guarding its approaches the mountains are rugged, of great altitude and of no value for agriculture or mining." He soon had 4,000 signatures on his petition and it looked promising. Steel and Tongue appealed directly to President Roosevelt. When the bill reached the House, it was vigorously debated. Tongue defended his position, stating that there was no value in the land. They made a few slight amendments to the bill, and then it was passed by the Senate. On May 22, 1902, President Roosevelt signed a law making Crater Lake a national park. The establishing act provided that the park was to be an area "dedicated and set apart forever as a public park or pleasure ground for the benefit of the people of the United States." The act required that measures be taken to preserve the scenery, timber, wildlife, and other natural features of the park for the use of "scientists, excursionists, and pleasure seekers."

Today, nearly half a million people from all around the world come each year to Crater Lake and stand in awe just as Hillman did so many years ago.

One

THE MOST BEAUTIFUL AND MAJESTIC BODY OF WATER

In October 1862, Chauncey Nye and his party of gold prospectors came across the crater. He later wrote that "the waters were of a deeply blue color, causing us to name it Blue Lake." After climbing one particularly rugged peak, the men named it Union Peak, in support of the Civil War. Nye wrote an article for the *Oregon Sentinel* describing the lake. This is the first recorded account of the lake.

John M. Corbell was part of Company I of the First Oregon Volunteer Infantry out of nearby Fort Klamath. In 1865, Corbell and 20 other men were building roads in Klamath County under the guidance of Capt. Franklin B. Sprague. One day when Corbell and F.M. Smith left the others and headed off to do some hunting out in the middle of nowhere, they came upon a huge lake. They quickly returned to camp and told the others. Days later, Captain Sprague led a group to see the lake. Upon seeing the lake, Sprague named it Lake Majesty.

Annie Stream and Annie Springs Campground were named for Annie Gaines Schwatka (1846–1876). Her brother-in-law, Maj. W.V. Rinehart, was a commander at Fort Klamath. In 1865, she accompanied him and some of the soldiers on an adventurous descent down to the water of Crater Lake. She is said to be the first white woman known to touch the water. She died in 1876, days after giving birth to her second child. Her time in Klamath County was remembered by a friend: "In that then wild land she was a great favorite, having commended herself to everybody by her intelligence and vivacity and by her kind and generous spirit. She had a very high appreciation of the beautiful in nature and was consequently an enthusiastic admirer of Klamath landscapes. She was an expert on horseback and was seen almost daily riding over the grassy plains and among the evergreen groves of Klamath land and no obstacle seemed too great for her to overcome when seeking to indulge her passion for adventure."

James Sutton (left) and David Linn (below) visited the lake in 1869. Sutton wrote, "Before us, and at our very feet, lay a large lake, encircled on all sides by steep and almost perpendicular bluff banks, fully as high as that we were standing upon. The circumference of the lake we could not estimate at less than 25 miles, and from the banks down to the water, not less than 3,000 feet. At no place could we see the remotest chance of being able to climb down to the water, without the aid of long ropes and rope ladders. Near the south end of the lake rises a butte island, several hundred feet high, and drifts of snow lay clinging to the crevices of the rocky banks. The waters were of a deep blue color, causing us to name it Blue Lake."

William Gladstone Steel is shown here. He wrote of the first time he saw Crater Lake: "As the journey draws to a close, and the last hill is being ascended, the excitement increases with each step. At last the darkness of the trees in front gives way to a glimpse of the blue sky, and a few minutes are sufficient to pass the last tree, when, instantly, Crater Lake, in all its glory, lies in full view at your feet."

Capt. George W. Davis, 13th infantry, who was in charge of the soldiers at Crater Lake in 1886.

Capt. George W. Davis was based at Fort Klamath. Fort Klamath was established in 1863 and served as an Army outpost during the Indian Wars. The government gave soldiers there the following duties: suppress Indian unrest, discourage harassment of travelers passing through the Klamath Basin, improve supply routes between eastern and western Oregon, and build new roads. Fort Klamath was closed in the 1880s when the wars subsided. Davis was with Steel when they launched *Cleetwood*. He was responsible for testing the effects of tension on the wire that was used to sound the lake.

Capt. Clarence Dutton, for whom Dutton Cliff is named, was also instrumental in launching *Cleetwood*. Dutton was born in Wallingford, Connecticut. He graduated from Yale in 1860 and remained there for the next two years while taking postgraduate classes. In 1862, he enlisted in the 21st Connecticut Volunteers. He went to work for the United States Geological Survey in 1875. He was in charge of the first geological study of the lake done in 1886 when they sounded the lake. He wrote of bringing the boats to the water: "With great labor the wagons were hauled up the incline over snow banks and through the forest until they rested upon the brink of the cliff which looks down into the lake." When early soundings revealed a depth of 1,210 feet, Captain Dutton became so excited that he asked a messenger to return to Fort Klamath and telegraph the world that Crater Lake was 1,210 feet deep.

The men are shown here in the *Cleetwood* in 1886. They took 168 sound recordings using a windlass that dropped weighted piano wire into the water to ascertain the depth. Each measurement was recorded, and then a signal was flashed via heliograph to the engineers standing on the Western Rim. They later changed the name of Western Rim to Watchman Peak to honor the work done that day. The men concluded that the maximum depth of the water was actually 1,996 feet.

The United States Biological Survey Party is pictured above. Members include Edward Prebble, Vernon Bailey, and Dr. C. Hart Merriam. Another member of the party, Dr. Frederick Vernon Coville, is pictured at right. In the late 1890s, he spent a week camping near the rim of Crater Lake with a group of botanists. They explored the area surrounding the crater, even venturing down to Wizard Island, all the while studying the various plant species that grow at Crater Lake.

Secretary of the Interior James R. Garfield is shown here on the way to Crater Lake in 1907. The party traveled via the southeasterly route between Klamath Falls and Crater Lake. Garfield is seated next to the driver. He was the first member of a president's cabinet to visit the lake.

During Garfield's visit, Steel changed the name of Castle Mountain to Garfield Peak to honor James R. Garfield, secretary of the interior. Garfield Peak is 8,060 feet high and towers 1,883 feet above the lake's surface.

The men pictured above include, in no particular order, Tom Chooktoot, Jack Palmer, Capt. Oliver Applegate, Reverend Kirk, Wosenkosket, Longjohn, Le-Lu, Chief George, Lole-To-Bux, and J.G. Pierce. Commissary Ivan D. Applegate is shown at right relaxing with his family. Applegate was asked to report to Klamath County to help settle the conflict during the Modoc Wars. He served as an interpreter and helped foster an agreement between the Indians and the white settlers. Years later, he helped with the Grande Ronde tribal status challenge.

Capt. Oliver C. Applegate is shown here with Dr. Colville. Steel named Applegate Peak after Captain Applegate for his work with the early explorations of the lake. Captain Applegate was born in Oregon in 1845; he was a son of Lindsay and Elizabeth Applegate. Lindsay and his brother Jesse came overland with their families in 1843. Each lost a son to the treacherous Columbia River while traveling. A few years later, the government asked them to find a better route for pioneers crossing the plains to Oregon. The Applegates accepted the challenge in the hopes that others would not have to endure what they had been through. They set out to blaze a trail into southern Oregon so that future travelers could avoid the treacherous Snake and Columbia Rivers. The men were successful in their endeavor, and thus the Applegate Trail, also known as the Southern Route, came to be. Over the next few years, thousands of immigrants followed the Southern Route on the final leg of their journey to Oregon.

Lt. Orson A. Stearns was with Captain Sprague when they first saw the lake. He recalled that they "reached the bluff overlooking the lake on the west or southwest side, about 9:00 in the morning of a clear day, and for the first time feasted our eyes upon what we pronounced the most beautiful and majestic body of water we had ever beheld." He wrote of venturing over the edge and making it all the way down to the water. Once at the water, he shot his gun in the air to assure the rest of his party that he was fine, as they were sure he was going to plummet to his death.

Upon seeing the lake for the first time, Capt. Franklin B. Sprague wrote, "You begin to comprehend the majestic beauties of the scenery spread out before you, and you sit down on the brink of the precipice, and feast your eyes on the awful grandeur, your thoughts wander back thousands of years to the time when, where now is a placid sheet of water, there was a lake of fire, throwing its cinders and ashes to vast distances in every direction." To describe the color, he wrote, "The appearance of the water in the basin, as seen from the top of the mountain, is that of a vast circular sheet of canvas, upon which some painter has been exercising his art. The color of the water is blue, but in many different shades, and like the colors in variegated silk, continually changing." In conclusion he wrote, "I do not believe any more majestic sheet of water is found upon the face of the globe, I purpose the name, Lake Majesty."

Captain Sprague is credited with naming this mass Phantom Ship due to its resemblance to a ship. It is said to be a phantom ship due to the fact that it can disappear from the scenery and not be seen again for a time. Poet Joaquin Miller wrote, "The one thing that first strikes you after the color, the blue, blue even to blackness, with its belt of green clinging to the bastions of the wall, is the silence, the Sunday morning silence. The plan now is to build a drive around the lake, so that these points can be considered in a single day from a carriage. And a great hotel is planned."

Zane Grey, a well-known writer, visited Crater Lake in June 1919. Upon seeing the lake for the first time, he wrote, "I expected something remarkable, but was not prepared for a scene of such wonder and beauty. Crater Lake was a large body of water set deep down in the pit of an extinct volcano. It seemed a blue gulf. Nowhere else had I seen such a shade of blue. This color was not azure blue or sea blue. How exquisite, rare, unreal! After a moment I seemed to think that it resembled the blue of heaven seen from the peak of a high mountain. This rare blue is not of the earth. Crater Lake had more similarity to an amethyst than any jewel I knew." Gray described watching the lake at the end of the day: "Then like magic it came. The most wonderful and beautiful of nature's transformations must be watched patiently. I saw a breeze rippling the waters of the lake. It changed the color, it darkened the blue."

In 1929, Edward Stuhl visited Crater Lake for the first time. In his journal he wrote, "Of all the color pictures I saw, and writings I read on Crater Lake, none does this marvelous jewel of nature justice. Coming up the hill and arriving at the abrupt crater rim the lake of a sudden and unexpectedly bursts into view, way down in an enormous bowl, a spherical sheet of such liquid deep purple-blue as I never credited in paintings, and yet those paintings compare dull with reality. Due to the white pumice and cinder deposits around the shallow shore of the island, the water plays in all nuances from emerald to ultramarine. The whole picture of Crater Lake touches on the phantasmic; the undulating crater rim appearing like a chain of mountain peaks, and ridges, and passes, contoured against the sky above and reflected in the water below, seems to float in an ether of transparent blue. And to the left, toward the west shore, rises—or seemingly floats—Wizard Island."

After visiting Crater Lake, John Muir wrote, "Met [Charles] Sargent and [Henry] Abbott at Ashland, and we immediately set out for Crater Lake, we three and the driver. The grades were steep and our horse feeble—one spotted roan with the colic and nervous debility, and the other grass-soft and balky and the spring wagon shakily but tough. Abbott wanted to turn back, but the team driver said it would soon be all right. Ash on the streamside, also alder and oak, the Kellogg and the white oak, with maple, grapevines, clematis, and glossy dark-green smilax climbing thirty feet up the alders. It was soon dark, and we saw the Douglas and yellow pines and the Murray pine in the starlight. Our astonished horses and driver ran point-blank against a clean shafted Pinus ponderosa. When we arrived at Hunt's, we found them gone to bed, but we drove into a cow corral and I built a fire. The wife arose and good-naturedly gave us an 11 o'clock supper."

Two

INCOMPARABLE IN BEAUTY

In 1911, famous writer Jack London arrived at the lake in a wagon pulled by horses similar to the ones pictured here. He later said Crater Lake was the most beautiful sight he had ever seen in all his travels. He said he was at a loss for words to describe it but summed it up as "incomparable in beauty."

Early visitors traveled via a wagon road that was built by the soldiers at Fort Klamath. The road linked Jacksonville to the fort. It came within three miles of the lake. Some came by foot, some on horseback, and others by wagon. Once the railroad reached southern Oregon in 1884, more people were able to travel greater distances to see this wonder that they had read about. From the train depot in Medford, they would travel by stagecoach to Klamath Falls. From there, they could take a wagon or go by horseback to see the lake.

In the early 1900s, if a person did not own an "automobile machine," he or she could enjoy the Crater Lake Company's daily automobile service between Medford and Crater Lake for $15. Automobiles left the Hotels Medford and Nash in Medford each morning, stopped for lunch in Prospect, and reached the lake in the evening. Returning automobiles left Crater Lake each morning, reaching Medford in time to connect with the outgoing evening trains. For $8.50 round-trip, the Crater Lake Company left the White Pelican Hotel in Klamath Falls each morning and arrived at the lake at noon. Returning automobiles left the lake after lunch and reached the White Pelican Hotel in time for supper.

These visitors are enjoying the view from what was known as Victor Rock (the Sinnott Memorial was built on that spot in 1931). The rock was named for Frances Fuller Victor, a historian of the Pacific west. Upon seeing Crater Lake, she called it Atlantis Arisen. There is also a meadow in the park named in her honor. Victor Rock posed quite a risk to visitors near the rim, due to the fact there was nothing protecting them from the edge.

The Flint automobile pictured here is making its way through a heavy layer of pumice dust, a reminder that a great volcano once occupied this area. The Flint was manufactured in Flint, Michigan, and was priced to compete with the Buick. One early visitor recalled, "One particularly bad spot on the road to Crater Lake was found at Pumice Hill, near the end of the journey. This hill is of pumice stone, and the dust on it is nearly a foot and a half deep. The grade is also very steep. On account of the dust, the clearance of the car would touch both coming up the hill and going down. The Inter-state car climbed the hill four times, three of the trips being to take the loads of other cars, stuck on the hill, to the summit."

The pinnacles were under sheets of volcanic pumice prior to the collapse of Mount Mazama. There are three main layers. The buff-colored bottom is approximately 80 feet thick and is composed of rhyodacite pumice and ash. In the middle is a gray layer about 80 feet thick and made of andesite scoria and ash. The top layer is approximately 10 feet thick and is composed of gray ash. The glacial striae have been studied at length over the years. Long before Mount Mazama erupted, the structure was covered in ice. The glaciers of Mount Mazama have left distinct records in the form of striae and moraines down the mountain slopes, as shown here.

When the National Park Service was created in 1916, construction and development of park facilities became the major focus. At Crater Lake, that meant construction of three new trails just in the first year. Prior to the creation of the National Park Service, there was no united agency in charge of the national parks. Some parks and monuments were under the Department of the Interior, others under the War Department, and still others were under the Forest Service of the Department of Agriculture. Pres. Woodrow Wilson signed the act creating the National Park Service to protect the nation's parks and monuments.

In the mid-1920s, a large-scale project called the Crater Lake Wall Trail got underway. There was a trail in existence, but it was difficult to navigate, with grades up to 28 percent. Plans called for this trail to be 8,000 feet in length, with grades no steeper than 15 percent. However, the one thing that was overlooked was the fact that in certain places, one section of the trail was above another section. This became problematic because of large rocks sliding down and injuring the people below. Yet another problem lay with the expense of opening the trail each summer and removing the large rocks and debris that had fallen during the winter. The trail was eventually abandoned.

The trails built in the early years led away from the rim and took visitors to parts of the park they would not experience otherwise. Shown here are men building the Discovery Point Trail in 1932. As Steel used to say, "What good is scenery if you can't enjoy it fully?"

The Rogue Elk Hotel in the Upper Rogue Valley near Trail opened in 1916 and provided respite for those traveling to Crater Lake. The hotel boasted 5,300 square feet with electricity, running water, 8 bedrooms, and 10 bathrooms. It took 90 tons of native rock to create two massive fireplaces in the hotel. Among the many guests were Pres. Herbert Hoover, actor Clark Gable, and writer Zane Grey. Further up the road was the Prospect Hotel. Prior to the hotel being built, travelers stopped at the Boothbys' house, hoping they could spend the night. The Boothby family owned a large house that looked very inviting to weary travelers. In 1892, they built a hotel, which allowed them to rent out 10 rooms.

Three

ANOTHER SKY LAY ALMOST UNDERNEATH OUR FEET

Early-day campers were asked to be considerate of the horse teams carrying people to and from the rim. There was a rule that "no camp will be made along roads except at designated localities. Blankets, clothing, hammocks, or any other article liable to frighten teams must not be hung near the road."

In the early 1900s, tent camps were provided for the comfort of travelers and their horses. In 1907, Steel, along with his partners Charles L. Parrish and Lionel Webster, operated a concession company at the park. The men acquired rights from the Department of the Interior to maintain permanent camps in the park. In July 1907, Tent City was set up near the present-day Crater Lake Lodge. That first year, 50 visitors took advantage of the accommodations. There was a kitchen available for the campers and feed available for their horses. At one time, a total of nine campgrounds existed, the most popular being that at the rim, where campers could sleep among the trees and wake up to beautiful sunrises over the lake.

The Cold Springs Campground was a popular spot for those wanting to sleep under the stars. Located nine miles from the rim, it was one of the first camping spots in the park. It was taken down in the 1960s. Steel is shown here with Capt. George Woodbury and Mike Taylor as they begin constructing a boathouse on Wizard Island in 1908.

As the number of campers increased, the demand rose to provide services for them. The comfort station pictured above was built in 1921. It provided running water and restroom facilities. At left is a comfort station that was built in 1928. It was 12 feet by 32 feet and had a common area and restrooms. The roof was made of logs and covered with shakes. The snow season of 1933–1934 proved too much for the structure; it was damaged beyond repair.

On September 1, 1888, Steel planted fish in the lake. Up to that time, there had never been any fish in the lake. He released 37 of an estimated 600 rainbow trout "minnows" that came from the Gordon Ranch out of Klamath Falls. In 1941, some 20,000 rainbow trout were planted in the lake. Between 1888 and 1941, many fish species were introduced, including brown trout, cutthroat trout, coho salmon, kokanee salmon, and several stocks of rainbow trout, including steelhead. Ranger Martin Johnson remembered a visitor asking him what he had in his bucket as he headed to the lake. Instead of saying he had a bucket filled with fingerling kokanee salmon, he replied, "This morning's blue dye for the lake!"

Steel wanted to have a grand hotel built that would rival the best lodges in Europe. He stressed that there would be "cleanliness, comfort, convenience, good food—well prepared and properly served." Construction got underway in 1909, but financial problems plagued the project from the start. Due to the short construction season, the work crept along summer after summer. Another problem was the difficulty in quarrying the rock for the walls and hauling it by wagon to the site. It soon became obvious that the cost to construct the lodge would far exceed the original estimate of $5,000. Steel advertised that when the lodge was completed there would be an assembly hall, a dining room that would seat 100 people, a massive stone fireplace in each of those rooms, immense fireplaces at each end of the lodge, a culinary department that would prepare first-class meals, and sleeping accommodations with all modern conveniences.

When the lodge opened, the cost to stay overnight with meals was $3.50. If one desired hot and cold water, the cost was an additional 50¢. It did not take long for the complaints to pour in about the shoddy construction. At one point, the park service director said, "The time has come to put accommodations at Crater Lake which will attract people instead of sending them away." A new concession company took over in 1921 and added a comfort station with hot and cold water, additional tent houses, and six eight-room cottages. A year later, the facilities received no complaints and showed a small profit

Edward Stuhl once wrote, "The Crater Lake Lodge overlooking the lake, it is an attractive 'rustic' building matching its natural surroundings, and, I do not agree with certain conservative persons who oppose such hostelries for, not every traveler and nature lover is able or in position to camp under a pine on the ground. However, crowds of tourists and especially automobiles I too do not cherish in nature's sanctuaries." In 1924, it was decided that there was a need for annexes at the lodge. Excavation began for the annexes, which were to mimic the older lodge. They used stone blocks for the first-floor walls, frame construction on the higher levels, and shingles on its roof and side. The interior rooms were furnished with iron beds, porcelain sinks, tubs, and toilets. The cost exceeded $100,000.

The cost to stay in the lodge during the 1930s was $1.50 for one person, with each additional person costing $1.25. However, if one wanted the comfort of hot and cold running water and meals, the cost was $4.25 per day for one person, or $22.50 for a week. Each additional guest paid $4 per day. The cost of a bath was 50¢. If a visitor wanted to enjoy a roaring fire in the fireplace, he or she had to spend an extra 25¢. A single meal could be had for $1. Saddle horses, pack animals, or burros could be rented for 50¢ an hour or $3 for the entire day. If one wanted his or her own personal guide, the cost was an extra $1 per hour or $3 per day. Rowboats were 50¢ an hour or $2.50 for the day. A round-trip boat ride to Wizard Island cost 50¢, or $2.00 to go to both Wizard Island and Phantom Ship. For $2.50, one could tour the entire lake.

As more people traveled to the park via automobile, more parking areas had to be created, as shown here. Parking was not a problem early on, as one visitor in 1911 recalled, "The superintendent of the park took our names, collected a dollar, and handed us a permit to use the roads of the park. The rules are simple. Automobiles are required to give warning at turns in the road and to keep to the outside of the grade. They are not allowed on the roads except between the hours of 6:30 and 10:30 in the morning and between 3:30 and 8:30 in the afternoon." He went on to say, "We made the start and chugged upward toward the blue sky. Then suddenly we gasped. Another sky lay almost underneath our feet. We were on the rim of Crater Lake."

The first superintendent of the park was William F. Arant. Prior to his appointment, he had been a rancher in Klamath Falls. His compensation for overseeing the park was $900 per year plus $100 to maintain his horse. He was allotted $2,000 per year in the beginning to maintain the park. These funds did not go far when there were roads to improve, trails to be built, and wages to be paid. One of Arant's first concerns was the roads. As park visitation continued to increase, Arant observed how wagons and automobiles cut into the road surface, making it into a "very fine and deep dust." He recommended that the road be thoroughly sprinkled with water since the very dusty condition of the roads constituted "the most disagreeable feature of traveling in the park." His office and residence are pictured.

Construction of a new superintendent's residence is shown here. The National Park Service advertised the position of superintendent by stating, "The park is located on the summit of the Cascade Mountains. The snowfall is very deep. It is a terrific task to open the roads and trails even by the first of July. The superintendent should have experience in snow removal, repair, and upkeep of roads and trails, and must be capable of selecting good men and holding them. He should also have experience in overhauling equipment, purchasing and handling Government supplies and materials, and using them efficiently and economically."

The first administration building, shown here, was an old log bunkhouse that was originally constructed around 1912 by Army engineers engaged in roadwork. For lack of other funds, it became home to the administration. Apparently, it was not an ideal setup, as one employee wrote, "Besides being too small, it is dark, cold, drafty, dirty, and verminous and a disgrace to the government." In 1933, $18,000 was allotted for a new administration building. The following spring, the old log administration building was razed to make room for the new building.

The new administration building measured 100 feet long and 40 feet wide. It was built from native stone so as to blend in with other buildings in the government camp area. The main floor housed the clerical department as well as offices for the superintendent, assistant superintendent, and the timekeeper. The building was completed in the autumn of 1935 and park personnel moved their summer offices into the structure in June 1936. Superintendent Canfield noted happily that the building "can be regarded as one of the most modern in any of the parks," and he observed that the "new headquarters supply sufficient room for park administrative activities, eliminating crowded conditions which had been such a handicap for years."

In 1949, the Crater Lake School Association was organized to handle the education of the employee's children who lived at the park year-round. The school was supported financially by parents, private funds, and donations. The school, which met in a room in the administration building, had five children in kindergarten and three in the elementary grades during its first year. One student, Judy Holmes, recalled her time growing up in the park: "It was living there and enjoying the amazing kaleidoscope of experiences that make it so special—the natural beauty, Mount Garfield keeping watch over our little community, Phantom Ship and the Old Man of the Lake, the moods of the lake, the depth and melting of snow, the woods, the canyons, the flowers, the waterfalls, and of course all the people who impacted our impressionable young minds." When she graduated in 1958 from Crater Lake School, she credited the teachers with making "two eighth grade graduates feel just as important as any kid in the city would have felt."

This building was originally the home of Kiser Photography Studio. Fred Kiser was a well-known photographer in Portland. In 1903, Kiser was recruited by Steel to take photographs of Crater Lake. Kiser, his assistants, and all of their photography and camping equipment required a team of 25 pack mules and two packers to make it to the lake. Since color photography had not been invented yet, Kiser hand colored each photograph. His reputation was at stake when people questioned why he had colored the water so blue. He assured them the water was truly that blue. His photographs of Crater Lake were exhibited at the 1915 Panama-Pacific International Exposition in San Francisco in the hopes of encouraging tourism. In 1926, he added a darkroom to the building, which allowed him to offer one-day film developing services for the tourists. He also installed coin-operated telescopes along the rim to give visitors a better view of the lake.

Early-day visitors enjoyed a truly rustic Crater Lake. When Oregon governor James Withycombe visited, he said, "I have tried several times to arrange a visit to the lake and each time something prevented, but now my fondest dreams have been realized and the beauty and grandeur of the lake far exceeds my expectations." Even though it was mid-June, his party had to shovel snow on the way up to the rim and then walk through snow, eventually arriving at 5:00 p.m.

During the 1920s, 12 cabins were built near the cafeteria. They were refurbished in 1941 along with the construction of additional cabins. The cabins were 12 by 16 feet, equipped with cold running water, oil heaters, electric lights, one double bed with linens and blankets, and two half beds with linens and blankets. Over the years, cabins have been constructed and remodeled in the Sleepy Hollow Area to house employees. The first dozen one-bedroom cabins were built in 1926. They replaced basic tents that had been there previously.

In 1931, a medical and first aid service for visitors and employees in the park was inaugurated, with Dr. K.N. Miller, head of the University of Oregon Health Service, beginning his duties as park physician for the summer in the building pictured. First aid tents were also set up to house patients being treated for minor injuries and illnesses. There was no hospital at the park when Doug Roach's daughter was about to be born. He recalled having to crank the telephone in 1937 to get through to a hospital in Medford. When he did reach a nurse, she shrieked, "Crater Lake! Get on your way in a hurry and take those curves easy!" When it was time for him to go back to work, a large snowstorm prevented his return. The nurses lent him a pillow and he slept in his car. Finally, the Roaches were able to return home with their newborn.

During the 1924 season, a community house was built on a site at the rim near Crater Lake Lodge. Boasting a large rustic fireplace, it was designed to house audiences attending nightly lectures and other entertainment during the tourist season. A Victrola, a brand of phonographs, was provided for the community house by the Medford, Oregon, Craters, a booster organization dedicated to the advertising and development of Crater Lake National Park. Shown here is the boathouse on Wizard Island. In 1915, there was only one boat in use. There was a second, half-finished boat, 36 feet in length, inside the boathouse. Truman Cook, age 22, and one of the house carpenters finished the boat. When it was time to install the 300-pound motor, it was gingerly brought down from the rim to the boathouse.

The headquarters pictured here were causing Steel a bit of grief in 1915. He wrote a letter to the government stating in part that "the park office has entirely outgrown its usefulness, in that it is totally inadequate for the purpose. The park office proper and the post office are located in a little room 8 by 12 feet, into which at times 40–50 people try to crowd and transact business. When the mail arrives on busy days it is simply a physical impossibility to transact business expeditiously or at all satisfactorily either to the public or the employees. A new modern building should be provided, as soon as possible, of sufficient capacity to meet all requirements for many years to come. The business is increasing rapidly and facilities for the systematic handling of it should keep pace therewith."

By 1927, it was apparent that there was a need for a cafeteria on-site. The concessionaire entered into an agreement to build and operate a cafeteria, a general store that would sell camping supplies, and some small rental cabins behind the cafeteria. By the time the season opened in 1928, all of the new buildings were ready for business. The cafeteria was open from 6:30 in the morning until 9:00 at night during the summer months. It advertised that "the same standard of meals may be secured at the cafeteria as at the lodge, and at reasonable rates."

As more and more automobiles came to the park, it was necessary to build a parking lot and, later, to landscape the area. Early on, there were many rules to follow if one wanted to drive an automobile in the park. For example: "When teams, saddle horses or pack trains approach, automobiles shall be so manipulated so as to allow safe passage for the other party. In no case shall automobiles pass animals on the road at a speed greater than 10 miles per hour. When automobiles going in opposite directions meet on a grade, the ascending machine has the right of way, and the descending machine shall be backed or otherwise handled as may be necessary to enable the ascending machine to pass in safety."

The workers here are paving a walkway in Rim Village. The name Rim Village can be attributed to Mark Daniels, the first general superintendent of national parks. Daniels visited Crater Lake in August 1914 to begin work on a model village similar to the one that he had planned for Yosemite National Park. Daniels's villages included sanitary water, telephone systems, electric lighting, and a system of patrolling the park (presumably by a newly created ranger force that he was advocating). He stressed that the locations of all buildings should be planned very carefully and the type of architecture should be studied prior to breaking ground.

The Sinnott Memorial is shown here. It was constructed in 1930 with funds from the federal government and the Carnegie Corporation of New York. The memorial was to honor Oregon congressman Nicholas J. Sinnott, a great supporter of Crater Lake. Building this structure, which sits 900 feet above the water, was an engineering feat. It was designed so that it would blend in with the scenery and not be seen from the lake. Today, Sinnott Memorial serves as a way for visitors from around the globe to learn about Crater Lake's history.

In 1926, a fire-lookout station was built on Mount Scott from plans provided by the US Forest Service. It was manned every summer. The Watchman Lookout and Tower was built in 1931. It was used to keep an eye on the 249 square miles of park. The first female lookout was hired in 1943 during World War II, when men were in short supply. The Watchman Lookout also served as a museum for the public.

The new Mount Scott fire lookout is pictured here. In 1940, a plan for a new fire lookout on Mount Scott was approved. However, there were delays in building the structure. In 1947, officials decided to add a storage space under the building, a gutter to supply water to a storage tank under the lookout room, and more equipment, furnishings, and appliances. Finally, the new structure was completed in 1952. Rangers working at either lookout stayed in communication with the fire dispatcher's office at park headquarters via shortwave radio and telephone.

The Civilian Conservation Corps (CCC) was created by Congress in March 1933. President Roosevelt had just taken office and was anxious to get the economy moving during the Great Depression. The program was aimed at men between the ages of 17 and 28. The pay was typically $30 per month, with $25 sent home. The CCC headquarters at Crater Lake is pictured here in June 1933. There were two CCC camps in the area. The first camp, known as Annie Springs, began at park headquarters but soon moved three miles south to Mazama Campground. The other camp, named Wineglass, was originally located closer to the rim. Camp Wineglass had CCC workers through October 1938. Camp Annie Springs kept working through the fall of 1941.

Each CCC camp could hold 200 workers, but they were not always at full capacity. Demands for workers at other locations as well as the workload at Crater Lake played a role in determining how many men worked at any given time. Most CCC workers slept eight men to a tent. The men were prohibited from drinking, gambling, and political activity. Those who left were not eligible to return to the CCC. Free vocational and academic courses were offered in the evenings. The men played sports in their free time. A CCC newspaper was published that highlighted work at Crater Lake.

William Bill Coulson recalled his time as a CCC enrollee: "Camp Wineglass was in a beautiful setting about 3 miles from the ranger station. We lived in tents with wooden floors and wooden sides about 4 feet high, heated with one small heater. There were about 250 men to a camp. Each one of these companies had a leader and an assistant, whose job it was to see that every man was up for roll call, breakfast at a certain time, beds made, tent cleaned, sides rolled up and ready for work detail on the grade by 7:30 a.m. Most of our work at Camp Wineglass consisted of roadwork, building roads so that fire trucks could get close to the fires. We built sidewalks up at the lake and also some log cabins, under supervision of Forest Rangers, all local men, all very good men. President Roosevelt and Robert Fechner visited Camp Wineglass briefly. We put on a show for them and their party. We had really good boxers and wrestlers and a championship baseball team."

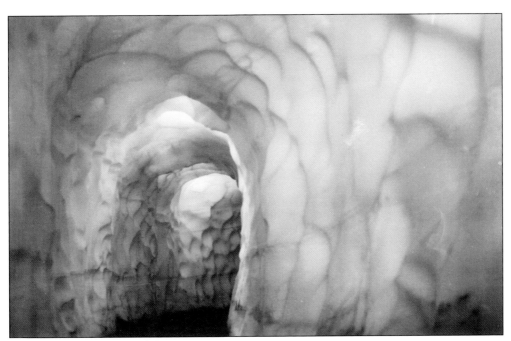

Probably nothing prepared the young CCC enrollees for the massive amount of snow they would encounter. Here, they have tunneled a path on the old rim road near the Watchman. Earl Wall remembers when he first arrived at Crater Lake after going down to the Jackson County Fairgrounds and signing up for the CCC program: "It was in the early spring, March or April. There was a lot of snow on the ground and we were just starting to build a new camp at Annie Springs when I got there. We had to dig out snow banks to set our tents and get things situated around so we could build a new camp. After we got that built, we started out on cleaning up along the roads, cutting a lot of snags and things that they quit doing later on."

The CCC men pictured here are preparing the soil for planting. First Lady Eleanor Roosevelt, along with her personal secretary, visited Crater Lake unannounced during August 1934. When she spotted the CCC men from Camp Wineglass working on landscaping the Rim Village area, she said, "A fine piece of work you are doing. Wherever I go, I hear so much of the good work you boys are accomplishing." By all accounts, First Lady Roosevelt enjoyed her stay at the park. Upon arrival, she asked a ranger if she could take a boat ride. Ranger Ernest Rostel was assigned to be her tour guide. They took a boat ride, had a personal tour of the park, and hiked the Lake Trail. She later wrote him a note of appreciation, "My dear Mr. Rostel: I want to thank you for the many services and kind things which were done for me while I was at the Pilot Butte Inn. It made my stay at Crater Lake most enjoyable and I am very grateful to you. Very sincerely yours, Eleanor Roosevelt."

The CCC built the Plaza Comfort Station pictured here. The CCC is credited with building a trail to Mount Scott and repairing the trails to Sentinel Point and the loop in the Castle Crest Wildflower Garden. Superintendent Arant's grandson, Howard Arant, recalled working at Crater Lake: "Another of my experiences in the park with the CCC boys that really comes to mind was building the trail up Mount Scott. It was all handwork. A lot of the outcroppings had to be dynamited to get the trail graded out as wide as it was supposed to be. I hauled lunches, tools, and dynamite up to that trail."

By the time the last of the CCC workers departed, roads had been built, fire lines had been constructed, new structures had been built, landscaping was completed, new trails were ready for hikers, new campgrounds welcomed visitors, and new signs hung throughout the area. Other major accomplishments by the CCC included water and sewer systems, as well as electrical and telephone lines. When the time came to disassemble the CCC camps, the main structures were removed, but the sites were converted to public campgrounds. Camp Annie Springs is part of the Mazama Campgrounds and Camp Wineglass began a new life as Lost Creek Campground.

Four

BEHOLDING THE SUPERBLY BEAUTIFUL SCENERY

The men seen here are beginning to build the first Rim Drive in 1913. The project was supervised by the Army Corps of Engineers. The workers were hired by the day rather than on a contract. One group went north toward Kerr Notch and then to the top of Anderson Point. The other group left from a permanent camp established in Munson Valley to reach the rim and then continued west.

The road survey crew worked long, hard hours. At the end of the day, they were ready for a good meal. Their camp consisted of six log structures with steeply pitched roofs, including a headquarters building, storage barn, blacksmith shop, aid cabin, and cook shack that housed a kitchen/dining room downstairs and a dormitory upstairs. The structures were clustered on both sides of the main road to the rim. Much of the construction was accomplished through either hand labor or horse-drawn road plows and graders. Progress in clearing and rough grading could be slowed, however, by the considerable amount of needed excavation by hand with picks and shovels in some places.

The Army Corps of Engineers wanted to build the "main highway" as close to the rim as possible. The average cost per mile was $13,000, but that did not include paving, which was an extra $5,000 per mile. Those prices did not include a guardrail either. Most years, crews operated from July to October. There were years when they were only able to complete three miles. They averaged between 50 and 100 men and between 6 and 15 horse teams. The steam shovel handled much of the rockwork, often after drilling and blasting, with finish grading done by hand and teams. During World War I, it was difficult to find available crews. Finally, after five years, the first automobiles were allowed to drive the entire Rim Road at the end of September 1918.

Early-day visitors had to enter the park via a single-lane, dusty highway that was barely more than a cleared path through the forest. One early visitor to the park, Edward Stuhl, recalled, "When the rim road is reached the going is easy and there are stopping places all along, offering vistas of Crater Lake. I photographed from a point between the Watchman and Glacier Peak. Here I experienced to be eye-and-ear witness in an incredible example of the acme of indifference; a fine car drove up; an elderly gentleman stepped to the spot where I stood on the crater rim and on beholding the superbly beautiful scenery before him begged his lady in the car to partake of the sight, but the dame refused to leave her comfortable seat."

Parking was not an issue when J.O. Shiveley became the first automobile driver to visit the park. His two-cylinder vehicle struggled over a road that was primarily for slow-moving wagons and horses. He had to negotiate deep ruts, dust, rocks, and narrow passageways. At times, horses had to help pull the vehicle over steep grades. It was another year before an automobile (operated by Charles Tru of Medford) drove under its own power all the way to the rim. Years later, another visitor recalled, "One particularly bad spot on the road to Crater Lake was found at Pumice Hill, near the end of the journey. This hill is of pumice stone, and the dust on it is nearly a foot and a half deep. The grade is also very steep."

The early 1930s saw many improvements to the roads. A new Rim Drive was built that followed the curvature of the lake better than the existing road. Also, a new road was built stretching from Government Camp to the rim. The new road's maximum grade was 6.5 percent, compared to the previous road's 11 percent grade. This was a far cry from when the early travelers traversed a wagon road. One visitor remembered what happened when the wagons were going in the opposite direction: "One of the older boys or a man would ride to the top or come down from the top to make certain the trail was clear and then fire a signal shot for the wagon to come up or down. Wagons on the way down would tie a log to the back to serve as a drag."

The new West Rim drive is under construction here in 1932. Due to the hard economic times, crews tried to do as much of the work by hand, thereby employing more men. Some of the men who were receiving financial assistance through Jackson and Klamath Counties were hired to do roadwork. The asphalt batch plant is shown here in 1938. This was a huge improvement to the early days of clearing rocks from the road to smooth the dirt for automobiles.

During World War II, all lodging and concession services were shut down due to gas rationing, rubber rationing, and the hard economic times. The number of visitors declined from 273,564 in 1941 to 27,656 in 1943 (6,392 of those were in the armed forces.) The permanent staff was reduced to nine, whose primary duty was to protect the park from fires during the summer months. All surplus trucks, tools, equipment and supplies were transferred to war agencies. All snow removal equipment was lent to the United States Army. The park concessioner suspended all public service operations in the park, including transportation, lodging, meals, and boat service. Once the war ended, visitors returned to the park, ready to relax after such a difficult time.

Five

THE GREATEST POSSIBILITIES OF ANY SCENIC PARK IN THE WORLD

William Gladstone Steel is pictured here. When he lived in Portland, he was the president of a climbing club named the Mazamas. When the club visited Crater Lake in August 1896, members realized the volcano that had once stood so tall did not have a name. They christened it Mount Mazama by breaking a bottle filled with water from the lake against a rock on the rim.

The duties of a ranger included enforcing regulations, protecting wildlife, patrolling roads and campgrounds, assisting visitors, preventing and fighting forest fires, controlling insects, supervising park entrances, compiling statistics, and overseeing communications. The ranger dormitory is shown here. By the end of a day, after dealing with medical emergencies, crime, poachers, wild animals, fires, complaints, questions and giving lectures on the history of the area, every ranger was ready for a good night's sleep.

The ranger dormitory (above) and the chief ranger's residence are pictured. The first floor of the ranger dormitory contained two living rooms, each with a stone fireplace. The larger room was for men, the smaller for women. There were three bedrooms and a shower for women on the south end. The remainder of the first floor included an entrance hall and four bedrooms, three with private baths. A basement lay under the central portion of the building. The second floor had four bedrooms, a large 18-by-34-foot dormitory room, a darkroom, storage room, and shower room. Many of the seasonal rangers were schoolteachers who worked at the park during their summer break.

Pictured here are the ranger's backcountry cabin and the old headquarters area. Ranger L. Howard Crawford recalled, "Not until the black bears had disappeared to their sheltered dens and the agile martens had become bold enough to flaunt their lustrous new coats before the eyes of man, did we consider winter really under way." Regarding living at Crater Lake, he said, "To the winter crew, all of whom had an appreciation for the beauty and wonder of our mountain fastness, the hardships which so often had to be met and endured, were mitigated and made bearable by Nature, in her gentle moods. Skiing and occasionally snowshoeing were our only means of locomotion for many months, principally between December and June. As a whole, the winter slipped away rapidly and now it is quite unbelievable to again see the earth uncovered."

The rangers and their motor fleet are pictured here in the early 1930s. One of the duties of a ranger during the snow season was to assist stranded motorists. Ranger Otis "Pete" Foiles remembered one such incident: "Helping people out when snow caused them problems was one of our duties. One morning I came upon a couple stranded on the road during a bad storm. They had been all night with no heat or a place to stay except in the car. When I stopped to help them I noticed we were right by a telephone that we had put up for just such situations. I asked them why they didn't use the phone to call for help. The fellow said, 'I thought about that, but the sign said For Emergency Use Only.' "

Pictured are Chief Landscape Architect Francis G. Lange (left) and one of his assistants, Vernon Bailey (below). Lange recalled, "Our approach to the landscape problem was to create everything in a natural environment as much as possible by the uses of materials, the skills of professional people we had, and the labor members that carried out these projects." He said, "This area was nothing but arid, volcanic soil which had constant erosion with no stabilization. All the soil, the topsoil and the sods, and plant material were obtained from Munson Valley. Many truckloads of material over a period of 1933 to 1939 were devoted in hauling material to the rim area to landscape it. The major landscaping was done in about 1940 and much effort was given to landscaping surroundings of the existing lodge and the cafeteria area."

John C. Merriam is pictured at right. Merriam was concerned that those visiting the national parks were "recreating instead of contemplating." He feared that people thought of the parks as playgrounds and were not willing to learn anything about their history. Therefore, he created the first educational programs at the national parks. The Stephen T. Mather plaque is shown below. Mather was the first director of the newly formed National Park Service in 1916. Upon visiting the lake he commented, "I have just come from the Crater Lake Park, and I am free to say that I believe it has probably the greatest possibilities of any scenic park in the world."

The naturalist's residence was completed during the 1932–1933 season. The naturalist program consisted of four principal elements: information, lectures, campfire programs, and guided trips. Naturalist Ted E. Arthur recalled his time at Crater Lake: "One of the fondest recollections of being at Crater Lake was the tremendous people that I met. We had square dances and things like hobo picnics, where we'd have to go out and beg a potato or an onion or a carrot. We'd generally have these out in the remote areas of the park. One was out there by Boundary Springs. We went out one evening and we had two giant garbage cans with stew in them and we sang. It was such a community type of experience, just like something you read about in books."

This sign advertises free auto-caravan tours led by professional naturalists. The naturalists at Crater Lake gave informative talks on the history of the park and educated visitors about the natural surroundings. In July 1931, a boat trip under the guidance of ranger-naturalists, described as "the only one of its kind in the world," was initiated. Visitors spent the entire day on the lake exploring Wizard Island, Devil's Backbone, and the Phantom Ship. Devil's Backbone is a vertical wall of dark andesite that appears as a conspicuous rib on the face of the cliff.

Many who worked at Crater Lake have fond memories of their time there. Janet Smith recalled how they would decorate a Christmas tree at the end of each summer season so they could have their own Christmas together before leaving for the winter. She spoke of the fun they had in the evenings listening to music, playing games, and relaxing. She remembered how much fun the Miss Crater Lake pageant was. She explained that one person from each department (housekeeping, food service, and so forth) was selected to compete in the contest. The management in turn chose the judges, who chose the winner. Miss Crater Lake received a small prize. Janet said preparing for the contest was half the fun—just trying to figure out how to make a long dress for $3 "called for a lot of imagination."

Calling Crater Lake home were a number of bears who had been encouraged to entertain the visitors. Sadie Roach remembered, "I did a washing and, of course, we had to put the line way up because the snow was so high. I hung these things out and I looked out to admire them, and what do you know, a great big bear was pulling each thing off the line." She remembered another time: "This day, I guess I didn't close the door too well. I went to put my mop in this mop closet and faced a bear, eye to eyeball, and it wasn't a very big place. He had come in, and turned around, and shut the door on himself. I was screaming out one door and he went right through the big window with four panes in it."

Shopkeeper Doug Roach recalled a young couple visiting on their honeymoon. They were asked if they had any food in their convertible automobile, but they denied having any. They went to explore the lake only to return to find the top to their convertible shredded by bears. They later said, "Oh, we didn't have any food. We just had some candy bars and oranges." Roach's wife, Sadie, remembered placing their baby outside in a bassinet in the afternoons. "After her bath I put her out there for her nap. I didn't know it, but everybody talked about me and said, she's not going to have a baby next year when we come." When they returned the following year they said, "Oh, you still have your little girl. We thought you wouldn't because you left it out with the bear."

Pete + Jeff's Lucky Day
Crater Lake National Park. - 340.

In 1912, Superintendent Arant thought it would be a good idea to feed and tame the bears in the park for the enjoyment of the tourists. Pete and Jett are shown here enjoying their afternoon snack. Below, Pete is feasting on a meal provided by the kitchen staff. Ranger Bernie Hughes recalled a bear they named Charity: "Charity liked people and sometimes was regarded as an unofficial greeter during the 1932 season, welcoming visitors to Crater Lake National Park. With all the dignity possessed by a two-year-old bear, she would station herself along the Western Entrance Road and await the arrival of motorists. During the early part of each morning and the later hours of the afternoon, she would sit on the pavement begging for food."

"Pete's Turn"
Crater Lake
National Park.
- 339 -

Although the original plan was to tame the bears for their entertainment value, by the late 1930s, the officials at Crater Lake realized the bears were becoming dangerous to the public. In years past, there had been an abundance of food left at the garbage pit by the CCC workers, road construction workers, and numerous visitors. Officials reported, "The bears, which have been spoiled for a good many years back by having ample food supplies, still hang around this pit, expecting to be fed, instead of getting out and rustling their own living. The result is that the bears have been hungry and as a consequence have been ill-tempered and more dangerous than at any time in the past several years."

Part of the staff pictured above includes, in no particular order, Elmer Applegate, Wayne Kartehner, and Ralph Huestis. All men worked as ranger-naturalists during the 1930s. Standing in front of the administration building below are Supt. Ernest P. Leavitt and his permanent staff, including, from left to right, Carlisle Crouch, Wilfrid Frost, Pete Foiles, ? Fitzgerald, Ernest P. Leavitt, Clyde Gilbert, and George "Doc" Ruhle.

The utility staff is shown above in front of the warehouse. Included are, in part, (first row) Dodge, Dick Finch, Dick Varnum, Ray Hale, Charlie Tru, Bill Beckman, Guy Hartell, and "Happy" Stradling; (second row) Norm Wimer, Harvey Cliff, Martin Palmer, and Clarence Hedgepeth. The naturalist staff are shown below in front of the administration building. Pictured are, in part, Joe Nee, George "Doc" Ruhle, Wayne Kartehner, ? Hodges, and Dr. Ralph R. Huestis.

The permanent (year-round) ranger force included, in no particular order, Wilfrid T. "Jack" Frost, Pete Foiles, Clyde Gilbert, and chief ranger J. Carlisle Crouch. They are standing in front of the administration building. The office personnel are shown below in front of the administration building. They include, in part and from left to right, (first row) Betty Vilm, Martha Grimes, Betty McCrae, and Gus; (second row) Mrs. Loren Miller, Raymond C. Strickler, Gladys Brewer, Charles Chrysler, and Ethel Wilkinson; (third row) Mabel Hedgepeth, Doug Roach, and Bernie Moore.

This photograph was taken a few years before Steel's death on October 21, 1934. Born September 7, 1854, Steel was the superintendent of Crater Lake from 1913–1916. When the National Park Service was established in 1916, he became park commissioner, a position he held until the time of his death. His daughter, Jean, then took over that post. At a national parks conference, Steel told the audience, "All the money I have is in the park, and if I had more, it would go there too. This is my life's work." In 1932, he told a friend, "I have accomplished that which I set out to do and now I am happy." Steel will always be remembered as the "Father of Crater Lake."

Six

CRATER LAKE HAS TWO SEASONS—WINTER AND THE MONTH OF JULY

Doug Roach remembered living at Crater Lake: "We improvised and we took it in stride and figured it was part of the life of living in the park. We enjoyed the summers and the fall. The summers were busy and hectic, but the falls and the springs were enjoyable, particularly the fall and the early winter months before the snow got awfully deep. It was just heavenly up there."

The question has always been what to do with all that snow. On average, the park receives 533 inches of snow (more than 44 feet) each year. The challenge is to remove enough of the snow to allow the visitors to reach the rim. The Rim Drive is generally closed from sometime in October until the following July. The road to the rim remains open for winter enthusiasts. It has been said that there are two seasons at Crater Lake: There is winter and the month of July. In 1909, a local newspaper reported that several heavy timber structures at Crater Lake collapsed due to a snowstorm that dumped 25 feet of snow in a short period of time. The structures included a residence, a barn, a shop, a toolshed, and some small miscellaneous buildings.

L. Howard Crawford was a ranger at the park during the 1930s. He wrote, "Exiled in such a world of beauty were five men, the winter crew, stationed at government headquarters, living and working through the long winter, recording snowfall and temperatures, maintaining telephone and power lines, painting, repairing, caretaking, photographing, and shoveling snow. Shoveling tons of snow, and during the long winter evenings, reading, narrating, developing photographs, listening anxiously and intently to the news and weather reports at the radio, or perhaps later in the evening to music and gaiety from some distant spot where all was light and laughter. But it was not always so. Sometimes it was a tortuous hell, battling foot by foot, ski shod, though miles of newly fallen snow in black weather, when returning from the monthly leave, seeking a break in the phone or power-line, or patrolling the headquarters area."

This panoramic photograph was taken in 1936 by United States Forest Service worker Lester M.

Moe. The image was taken from the Watchman Lookout.

Ranger R.P. Andrews told of a snow tunnel that stood 18 feet tall on opening day, June 15, 1933. It was the creation of the new snowplows and it drew a lot of attention from the public. He recalled, "Once a mother bear with three small cubs essayed to climb the dizzy heights on top in a vain search for food. A crowd at the checking station stood breathless as the old lady ambled over the span, the three cubs following in single file. Would it hold them up, or would they crash through? At this crucial point, a man came out of the front door and through the tunnel. Much to his amazement, he was greeted with gales of laughter. He did not realize that to the others it looked like a game of 'heavy, heavy hangs over thy head.' Finally, the bear family, in disgust, wandered away, and our tunnel remained intact. Several rangers showed signs of disgust, too. It had been the picture of the year, and nobody at Annie Springs could find a camera."

The mess hall is shown buried under snow. The winter caretaker spoke of a storm in 1924–1925 that rattled the lodge: "The fourth floor was like the deck of a ship in moderately rough weather. The fierce winds blew hard enough that there is hardly a square foot on the storm side that the snow does not find its way through." Hazel Frost recalled, "The privilege of living in a place like that was paramount. It much outweighed any of the hardships that were there. The people that we got to know there have lasted a lifetime as friends. We wouldn't give that up for anything. I suppose that is one reason why I feel special about Crater Lake."

It has been said that spring has arrived when enough of the snow has melted to expose the *Lady of the Woods*. The three-foot-tall sculpture (not pictured) was carved out of a boulder by Earl Russell Bush, who was a 31-year-old medical doctor who spent the summer of 1917 working on the road crew that built the first rim drive around Crater Lake. The season's work had largely ceased by the end of September 1917 and he found himself with almost two weeks of free time, so he carved his first-ever sculpture. Years later, he explained his desire to create the work: "This statue represents my offering to the forest, my interpretation of its awful stillness and repose, its beauty, fascination, and unseen life. A deep love of this virgin wilderness has fastened itself upon me and remains today. It seemed that I must leave something behind."

Ranger Otis "Pete" Foiles remembers winter: "I proposed to my wife at Cloud Cape Overlook in August 1940. We were married October 15, 1940, and moved into our 'Honeymoon House' at Park headquarters area. Our first child, Elouise, was born in April 1942 and we had to put her in a toboggan to get to our house upon our return from the hospital, because a snowstorm had closed the road. Of course, snow was a big experience for us. We were used to snow in Colorado, but not the amount that we got at Crater Lake. At that time, only about 10 families lived in the park in the winter and we became one big family. We were very comfortable under 25 feet of snow, but when the power went out for two or three days it was a challenge because we used electricity for cooking. We would end up cooking on top the oil stoves that were used for heating the houses. I think the lake is even more beautiful in the winter than in the summer."

During the 1920s and 1930s, the annual Snow Carnival was held. The activities included snow balling, short races, tobogganing, sleigh rides, barefoot races, sled dog races, and a homing pigeon race. There was also a dance held in the community house. From the haphazard way in which the vehicles are parked, it seems that everyone was in a hurry to get there. Myrtle Copeland was in such a hurry to get to the first snow race in 1927 that she forgot one small thing: her ski boots! Undeterred, she skied in her bedroom slippers. She did not win that year, but nine years later she took first place in the woman's category. The event continued to draw huge crowds. An estimated 3,500 spectators enjoyed the events in 1931. That number climbed to 4,000 people in 1933.

Beginning in 1927, the Crater Lake Wilderness Race took place annually. Skiers raced 42.6 miles between the lake and Klamath Falls. The route climbed in elevation by 2,200 feet. The first year, 24 skiers entered the race. The *Klamath Falls Herald* referred to the race as "one of the greatest battles of endurance, of wits, and of the elements in the history of the Pacific Coast." Manfred Jacobson of McCloud, California, finished first after a grueling 7 hours and 34 minutes. He won $250. Emil Nordeen won the race in 1929 and 1931 (he came within 34 seconds of winning the race in 1930.) Nordeen received an impressive 38-inch-high cup made of solid silver with gold trim after his second victory completing the race in 5 hours and 35 minutes.

After the 1935 race, the *Klamath Falls Herald* reported that "skiers and officials of the Crater Lake Ski Club and Klamath Winter Sports Association are inclined strongly to the opinion that the long race is too tough, and now that Hedberg, by virtue of his two victories, has won the cup, the event might as well be dropped from the Klamath winter sports program." The race was thereby shortened to five miles in 1936 and 1937. Frank Drew of Klamath Falls and Delbert Denton of Fort Klamath were the winners those two years. A race of only one mile in length was held at the rim of Crater Lake in 1938. That was the last year the race was held.

Another popular sport was ski jumping. Control of snow sports and the participants themselves made it necessary to hire more rangers. According to Chief Ranger Crouch, the "size and number of snow sports areas consistent with the use must be controlled, as must the ski trails, snow fields, cross country trips, and the actions of people anywhere near the rim of the lake, on the highways and elsewhere." Aid to injured persons as a result of snow sports activities was also a major component of the rangers' duties.

The record ski jump of all time was 151 feet. The ski jump was located adjacent to the present-day Annie Creek Snopark, just south of the park boundary. Crater Lake was second to only Mount Hood for winter sports. In 1946, the park was open year-round after being closed during World War II. That year, a gasoline-driven ski tow was installed in the bowl below the lodge. The rope tow was approximately 900 feet long and carried skiers to the summit of Knob Hill. Before the war, various rope tows had been set up for skiers, but this one was more professional. The concessioner who ran the rope tow also offered a gasoline station, a cafeteria, and limited overnight accommodations in the cafeteria building.

During the 1933 Snow Carnival, thousands of people crowded into the park to welcome Scotty Allan of Nome and his dog team of Alaskan huskies. This was the first year the dog race was held. Allan had won other competitions with his team of 15 dogs, but this was his first time competing in the 32-mile race on the rim of Crater Lake. The team came in at five hours, winning the first-ever mushing competition.

One of the problems that resulted from the winter closure of the park during World War II was the damage done to the roads and buildings from the snow not being removed. Crater Lake operated with just a skeletal crew during that time. The park had to loan all of its snow removal equipment to the United States Army during the war. Despite the deferred maintenance, a decision was made to open the park year-round after the war. Two years later, officials from the National Park Service visited the park to study the feasibility of offering permanent downhill skiing. After studying various possible sites, they concluded that the long-term expenses outweighed the benefits. They decided instead to promote the area for cross-country skiing and snowshoeing.

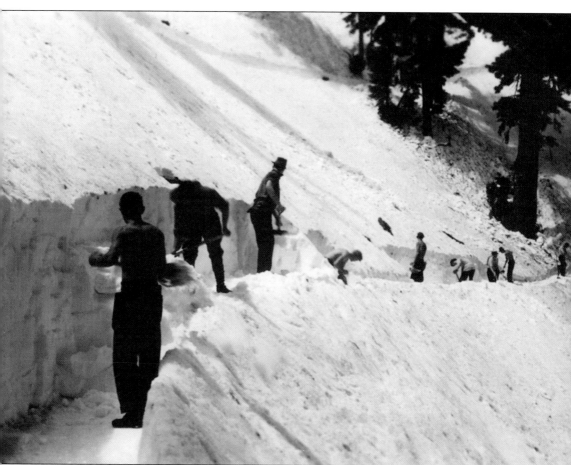

Sometimes, the best way to clear the snow is just an old-fashioned shovel. It 1927, it was reported that "snow removal, especially during years of heavy snowfall, was a major undertaking of park maintenance crews. For instance, the winter of 1926–1927 witnessed a total snowfall of more than 51 feet, the snow being heavily compacted by spring thaws. This amount of snow was difficult to remove, since there was no mechanical snow removal equipment available. To permit visitors to enter the park, it was necessary to clear more than 15 miles of heavy snow by using explosives and shovels. This gargantuan feat was finally completed on July 2, thus causing the park's 1927 summer season to commence five weeks later than the year before."

The snow was still causing problems in 1929. The superintendent wrote a letter to the National Park Service that reads, "There is no mechanical snow removal equipment in this park, and it becomes necessary each spring to expend considerable sums for labor to clear our roads of snow in time for the opening date. The roads of the park were opened this season on the following dates: Klamath-Medford Loop, June 12; Annie Spring to rim, June 22; east entrance, June 24; north entrance, July 6; Rim Road, July 13." Finally, in 1930, the park acquired a new "mechanical snow remover." The superintendent reported, "With its use the road to the rim from both the south and west entrances was open to traffic on May 24, the earliest opening date in the history of the park. The north entrance and Rim roads were open to travel on June 26, the earliest that either road had been opened."

The following year, the park hired two snowplow operators at a salary of $100 per month each plus board. The two men managed to plow 909 miles of pavement in the park for a total cost of $2692.40, which included labor and expenses relating to the equipment. They reported, "The new snow plan has proven the theory that it is much easier and more economical to remove the snow while it is still soft or following each of the winter storms rather than to wait until spring when the snow becomes packed and almost solid ice. The plow could travel between a quarter of a mile up to 15 miles per hour. The plow consumed an average of nine gallons of gasoline an hour. During the 1931–1932 seasons the plow used 10,009 gallons of fuel. It also used 159 of oil and 376 pounds of grease."

Ranger Richard M. Ward remembered what it was like to clear snow from a roof by hand: "The routine was as follows: up in the morning, after some discussion as to who would get up and build the fires and start breakfast (hot cakes and bacon). After breakfast, snow removal. We divided the roof into sections and shoveled trenches all the way to the roof, eave to eave and over the top; then using a saw, sections were cut off and rolled clear of the roof. This soon becomes back-breaking work. The snow removal continued all day, with short breaks for coffee and lunch. As soon as it started to get dark we had dinner of wieners, potatoes, peas, biscuits with butter and jam, and peaches, all washed down with lots of coffee. We all hit the sack early to rest our sore and tired muscles."

During the 1930s, Harry "Happy" Fuller worked as a snowplow operator. He remembered his times with "Betsy the Plow": "When it starts snowing we wait, until there is a foot of snow on the road before we start plowing. We must then continue to plow through the storm and for approximately four days afterwards before the roads are clear. It is not unusual to plow for 36 hours without a break; then a hasty meal, a couple of hours sleep and back to plowing. This seems more credible when the violence of our storms is known. For instance, in one storm this winter that lasted for 11 days, 13 feet, 9 inches of snow fell. After another storm that lasted for one day, we found 35 inches of fresh snow on the roads. And then perhaps there only will be one clear day before the start of another storm. From this you can see that Betsy and I are pretty close companions. There is something binding about facing a fury of driving snow and sub-zero temperatures together."

The "mechanical snow remover" arrived in time for the record-setting snowfall of 1931–1932. The officials at Crater Lake reported, "The winter of 1931–1932 taxed the park's snow removal capabilities to the limit. All known records of snowfall in the park were broken as 65 feet of snow fell at Government Camp and between 85 and 90 feet fell at the rim. Despite the heavy snowfall the park was able to keep the upper sections of the park roads, from the Rim to points below Annie Springs towards both the west and south entrances, open all winter with one rotary snowplow. It required two crews of two men each working almost constantly during the months of December and January to remove the snow from the upper park roads. During those months the plow was operated continuously for 117 eight-hour shifts, an average of approximately sixteen hours per day."

In 1937, Superintendent Canfield reported on the merits of snow removal: "Up until the acquisition of powerful snowplow equipment, the wonders of Crater Lake during winter months were viewed only by the eyes of persons who skied or snowshoed over 20–25 miles of snow. The park was practically inaccessible from November until late June or July 1. Snow was removed entirely by hand labor, making only a one-way traffic lane possible. The one-way traffic would persist until after the middle of July." The previous year, the park's one and only snowplow broke down and a part had to be ordered from Dubuque, Iowa. It arrived by rail to Chiloquin, but by then, there had been 19 days of steady snow and no plow.

During the winter of 1935–1936, it was decided that the park should be open year-round due to the success of snowplowing. Keeping the park open all winter meant that more rangers had to be hired. The park used temporary personnel until the winter of 1938–1939, when it was able to hire two permanent rangers. Even with the additional personnel, Superintendent Leavitt reported that the winter ranger staff was "not adequate to handle checking, road patrols, trail and boundary patrols, and numerous emergency calls." He explained, "On weekends of heavy travel of skiers, it was necessary to accept the volunteer services of members of ski clubs to patrol ski trails, and to call on the assistance of ranger personnel from the Lava Beds. The entire ranger staff was able to apply on numerous occasions the Red Cross First Aid training which they received during the fall and early winter months, several serious accidents and numerous minor accidents occurring among the skiers."

Permanent ranger Rudy Lueck is enjoying a moment in the snow in this photograph. Permanent ranger Charles H. Simson recalled working at Crater Lake during the winter: "January found us in a turmoil endeavoring to remove the snow from the roads and to keep the necessary building open. Spending the night out in blizzards, blasting our way through huge drifts and snow slides to make way for the snowplows became common, and the banner month of the season soon passed, adding 15.5 feet to our total. We became so used to great depths of snow that to pass around the summer cottages and see nothing but mounds of snow or a part of an upper window barely showing did not greatly impress us."

The winter of 1949 was so cold that Crater Lake froze over. It is rare for the lake to freeze due to the depth of the water, but it has happened from time to time. Duane "Do-We" Fitzgerald, Crater Lake National Park's acting chief ranger, and George "Doc" Ruhle, the park's chief naturalist, climbed down the caldera walls and walked across the frozen lake to Wizard Island. Years later, Ruhle recalled, "Several hundred feet from shore the ice began to crack and rumble ominously and numerous tests were made of its strength. Finally, about 1,000 yards out, under a cover of only four inches of snow, I succeeded in chopping through the ice, and with my thumb and index finger, estimated it to be two inches thick. The hole was enlarged to admit a snowshoe, which could be shoved three to four feet into the water beneath. This confirmed that the ice cover was on the lake water itself, and not over a pocket of surface ice."

In December 1950, the park received 313 inches of snow, 73 inches of which came down in 48 hours. This photograph was taken on February 5, 1951. A month later, it was reported that there was 177 inches of snow on the ground. By the time the last of the snow had fallen in June of that year, the park had received 835 inches of snow.

This panoramic photograph, taken by Lester M. Moe, shows the lake in 1936. In addition to the Phantom Ship, there are two other points of interest. Wizard Island is a volcanic cinder cone that rises approximately 763 feet above the lake. The entire area is approximately a square mile. There are other cinder cones in the lake, but this is the only one visible above the water. Wizard

Island formed when lava built up from the small eruptions that took place after Mount Mazama collapsed. In 1896, a member of the United States Geological Survey party, Joseph Silas Diller, reported "finding a broken off tree floating upright in 37 feet of water near Wizard Island." Known today as the Old Man of the Lake, the tree continues to keep watch over the lake.

DISCOVER THOUSANDS OF LOCAL HISTORY BOOKS FEATURING MILLIONS OF VINTAGE IMAGES

Arcadia Publishing, the leading local history publisher in the United States, is committed to making history accessible and meaningful through publishing books that celebrate and preserve the heritage of America's people and places.

Find more books like this at
www.arcadiapublishing.com

Search for your hometown history, your old stomping grounds, and even your favorite sports team.